WILD HORSES

GALLOPING THROUGH TIME

KELLY MILNER HALLS
ILLUSTRATIONS BY MARK HALLETT

Dedication

To the masters of resurrection at Darby Creek—Susan Copp and Randy Asmo—who saw the world shatter and found the will to help put it right. Thank you for helping me tell this story even if the path was at times a little rocky. You made miracles happen. And to the goddess, Tanya Dean—here's to the next chapter!

Text copyright © 2008 by Kelly Milner Halls
Design copyright © 2008 by Darby Creek Publishing

Cataloging-in-Publication

Halls, Kelly Milner, 1957—
Wild horses : galloping through time / Kelly Milner Halls ; with illustrations by Mark Hallett.
   p. ; cm.
ISBN 978-1-58196-065-5
Ages 11 and up.— Includes bibliographical references and index. — Summary: Introduces the horse family tree including the relatives of today's modern horse that are now extinct, as well as the species of zebras and asses that still live in the wild.
1. Equidae—Juvenile literature. [1. Horse family (Mammals)] I. Title. II. Author. III. Ill.
QL737.U62 H35 2008
599.665/5 dc22
OCLC: 209853279

Darby Creek Publishing
7858 Industrial Parkway
Plain City, OH 43064
www.darbycreekpublishing.com

Photo Credits: cover: wild horses in desert © Eastcott Momatiuk/Getty Images; wild horses in cloud of dust © Kathi Lamm/Getty Images. 15: Przewalski horse © Dreamstime. 17: Przewalski horses © Kateryna Slivinska. 18: tomb of Nikolai Przhevalsky © Svetlana Shevelchinskaya. Przewalski horse grazing © dreamstime; Przewalski horse face © Dreamstime. 20: Przewalkski horses © Kateryna Slivinska. 21: Chernobyl Przewalski horses © Sergey Starostenko/Landov. 22: Przewalkski standing in road © Dreamstime. 23: Przewalski horses © Kateryna Slivinska. 24: two kiang © Xinhua /Landov. 26: onager © Dreamstime. 27: nomadic tribe © Dreamstime. 28: Sorraia horse © Leslie Town—Leslie Town Photography/courtesy of Lynne Gerard. 29: Tarpan © Dreamstime. 34: horse painting © Dreamstime. 36: Uffington Horse © Dae Sasitorn/Last Refuge Ltd. 38: Caspian horse © Francie Stull. 39: Caspian horses © Francie Stull. 40: Caspian horses © Francie Stull; Caspian horse © Francie Stull. 41: Caspian Horses © Francie Stull. 42: Arabian horses © Dreamstime. 44: U.S. Army Captain William Sumner/courtesy of William Sumner; Arabian horse/courtesy of William Sumner. 45: Arabian horse rescue/courtesy of William Sumner; veterinarian check/courtesy of William Sumner. 46: Namibia horse © FLPA/Alamy. 47: Grevy twins © Dreamstime; plains zebra stripes © Dreamstime. 50: zebra stamp courtesy of the South African Post Office. 53: Namibia horses © TS Corrigan/Alamy. 56: mustang © Dreamstime; Abaco Barbs © Arnd Bronkhorst Photography. 57: mustangs © Dreamstime; mustang in flowers © Dreamstime. 58: herd of mustangs © Dreamstime. 62: horse family © U.S. National Park Service. 63: herd of horses © U.S. National Park Service. 65: group of mustangs © Dreamstime; mustang running through water © Dreamstime. All other photos from royalty-free stock sources are not credited.

Printed in the United States of America
2 4 6 8 10 9 7 5 3 1

CONTENTS

SMALL BEGINNINGS: PREHISTORIC HORSES

Horses. When you watch them from a distance—galloping across open acres, nuzzling their herd-mates, sleeping peacefully in the morning sun—they seem strong and graceful and diverse. When you look at them close-up, you see the tenderness in their eyes; you see intelligence, loyalty, even trust.

This blend of power in body and spirit has made the horse a mystical animal in legend and literature and a steadfast friend to mankind. Thousands of years before human and beast joined forces, the horse resembled the family dog in stature. Ancient horses started small, then evolved into the animals we know today.

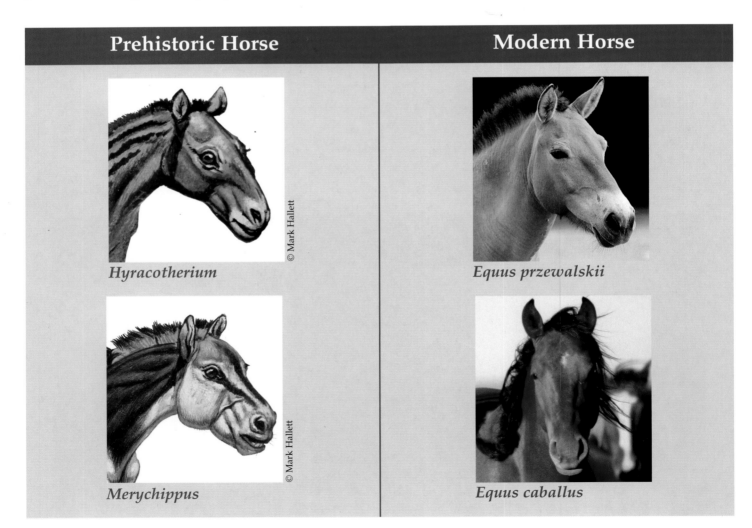

Prehistoric Horse	Modern Horse

Hyracotherium

© Mark Hallett

Merychippus

© Mark Hallett

Equus przewalskii

Equus caballus

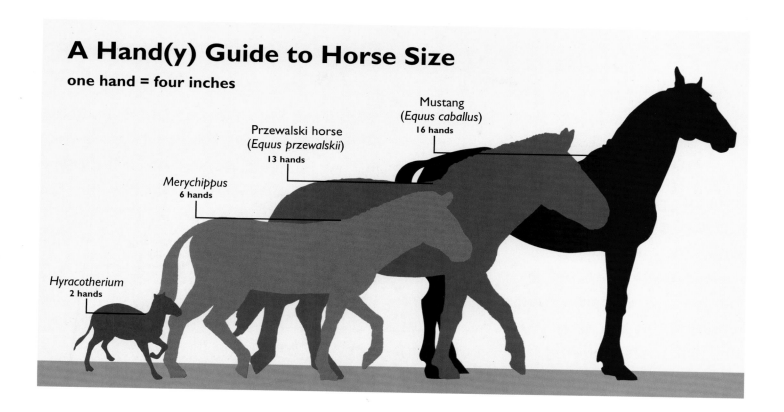

A Hand(y) Guide to Horse Size

one hand = four inches

Mustang
(*Equus caballus*)
16 hands

Przewalski horse
(*Equus przewalskii*)
13 hands

Merychippus
6 hands

Hyracotherium
2 hands

GIVE ME A HAND WITH HORSES

Modern horses (and most ponies) are measured from the withers—the horse equivalent of human shoulders—to the ground at hooves. But they aren't measured in feet or even in inches. They are described in increments called "hands"—each hand equals four inches.

Why hands? Because when horse traders first began to exchange their animals for money or other goods—possibly in ancient Egypt—they would compare the size of horses by laying a hand against the ground, palm flat against the horse's hoof, fingers pointing toward the head or tail of the horse. Next, they would lay their second hand horizontally on top of the first—and that was a full two hands. They repeated that process, counting each hand, until they reached the horse's withers.

It was an easy way to make the measurements without finding a tool. But hands weren't always accurate. A woman's hand might be smaller than the hand of a man, for example. A child's hand might be smaller than a woman's. So at some point, probably about five thousand years ago, a "hand" measurement was converted to a standard size, just to make it consistent, no matter who did the measuring. This age-old way of measuring a horse is still used today.

HYRACOTHERIUM: THE FIRST HORSE

The first true horses, *Hyracotherium* (or *Eohippus*, "dawn horse"), would have measured eight to nine inches (two hands high) from the ground to their withers.

Human beings were millenia away from taking their first breaths, but if we could go back in time to observe the tiny horses that galloped across North America, their size wouldn't be the only thing we'd find surprising. *Hyracotherium* had four separate hooves on its front legs: one on each of four toes. Each of its back legs had three hoofed toes.

What was life like for the little wild horses? The climate in the northern hemisphere was tropical and lush, like a modern-day rain forest near the equator. The greenery was thick in this hot, humid world, so food for leaf-eating grazers like *Hyracotherium* was plentiful. But danger also lurked at every turn.

Dinosaurs had disappeared by the time *Hyracotherium* appeared. But other predators had taken their place: carnivores like the deadly, flightless bird *Diatryma*, which, at six feet tall, towered over the tiny horse.

Hyracotherium traveled in herds, searching for leaves and berries to fill their bellies. But the protection of numbers proved no match for the razor-beaked *Diatryma*. Although it couldn't fly, *Diatryma* could easily outrun the

© Mark Hallett

Hyracotherium

small horses and snatch them up, like flightless hawks gobbling mice. Weighing more than two hundred pounds, these bulky birds could easily trample the horses.

Drinking fresh water at the river's edge was no easier than browsing for greens. Stalking, near motionless in the water, were the *Eocene*, cousins to crocodiles, and the four-legged mammal, *Ambulocetus*—which would eventually evolve into an early whale. In one sudden rush, either hungry carnivore would leap into action. It was a fearful, perilous life.

In the end, the odds were against tiny *Hyracotherium*, and it followed the dinosaurs

© Mark Hallett

Hyracotherium was defenseless against predators like *Diatryma*.

into extinction about forty-five million years ago. But other prehistoric horses were ready to move forward on the trail.

The Name Game

Famed British dinosaur scientist Sir Richard Owens named the fossil *Hyracotherium* in 1841. When American dinosaur hunter Othniel C. Marsh found fossil evidence of the same prehistoric horse in 1876, he thought he'd found a new species and named it *Eohippus*, which has become a very popular nickname. Because Owens named it first, *Hyracotherium* is the official scientific name.

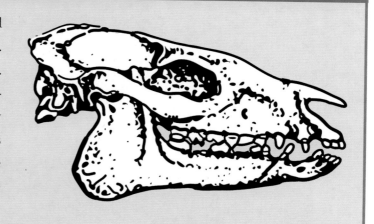

MESOHIPPUS: THE GRAZING HORSE

From thirty-seven to thirty-two million years ago, *Mesohippus* or "middle horse" appeared in the fossil record, again in North America. This prehistoric horse was still small, but outgrew *Hyracotherium* to stand two feet (six hands) high, with a long tail roughly one third of its full body length.

Its face was slightly longer and its eyes were rounder and set farther apart—making it look more like the modern-day horse. Even its teeth were evolving to include grinding molars. Those molars made it possible for *Mesohippus* to graze on grass and browse on leaves and berries. The diverse diet made it easier for the little horse to survive.

Where *Hyracotherium* had four toes (and four hooves) on its front feet, *Mesohippus* had only three. *Hyracotherium* carried its weight more or less evenly on all four toes. But *Mesohippus* balanced its weight on its middle front toe, a trait which eventually led to the single hoof we see on horses today.

Ancient jungles began to thin, thanks to increased volcanic activity. Saber-tooth cats became the primary predators, hunting the weak and the elderly among the herds. In time, *Mesohippus* went extinct—about thirty million years ago.

© Mark Hallett

Mesohippus

MERYCHIPPUS: THE FASTER HORSE

Though many other prehistoric horses lived between the extinction of *Mesohippus* and *Merychippus*, we focus on this species because it represents at least two special milestones in the evolution of the domestic horse. Standing four feet (12 hands) tall, *Merychippus* was the first prehistoric horse to develop long, swift legs and a much larger brain to help it escape predators and migrate in search of seasonal grasses. Now a full-fledged grazer, *Merychippus* depended upon its ability to find new sources of grass to survive.

The long face and prominent jaw that define the look of the modern horse were also common to *Merychippus*. And while it still had three hoofed toes on each foot, the center toe carried the bulk of *Merychippus's* weight. In time, the other two toes barely touched the ground.

Saber tooth cats still had a taste for horse flesh, but thanks to *Merychippus's* physical advances, fewer fell prey to the menacing predators.

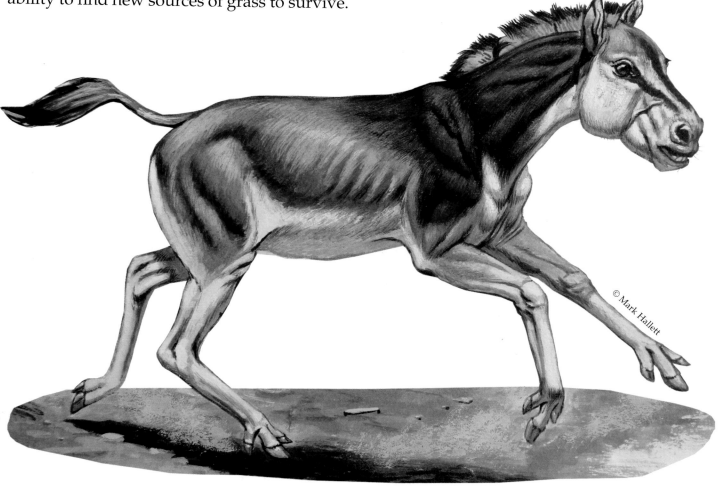

© Mark Hallett

Merychippus

Interview with Dr. Jerry Hooker

Dr. Jerry Hooker works as the Manager of the Vertebrates and Anthropology Division of the world famous Natural History Museum in London, England. His favorite arena of study is the realm of mammals—how they evolved and how their natural environments influenced that evolution.

With decades of research behind him, he was the obvious choice to advise the BBC/Discovery Channel producers of *Walking With Prehistoric Beasts*—the sequel to *Walking With Dinosaurs*—when it came to simulating prehistoric mammal lifestyles on the popular documentary.

We caught up with Dr. Hooker and asked him a few questions about his work with prehistoric horses.

Halls: Where have the best early horse fossils been discovered?

Dr. Hooker: The most complete and abundant specimens have been found in the western U.S. The Bighorn Basin in Wyoming is a classic area for *Hyracotherium* fossils. An important early find of a partial skeleton, however, was made in the 1850s at Harwich, Essex, U.K.

Halls: What made those fossils so amazing?

Dr. Hooker: They are so much smaller than modern horses (dog-sized) and have such different ecological adaptations. They had three to four hoofed toes on each foot and fed on soft leaves and fruits, much like modern chevrotains in Southeast Asian forests.

Halls: How can you tell this is an ancient ancestor to the modern horse? What traits do they have in common?

Dr. Hooker: They share similar anklebones and some small but critical similarities in the skull and teeth. The skull and tooth features originally went unnoticed in the nineteenth century, and it is really the long sequence of fossils from the last fifty-five million years in the U.S., showing gradual evolutionary changes towards modern horses that made scientists realize that these small mammals are ancestral horses.

Halls: Why didn't any of the smaller ancient horses survive to modern times?

Dr. Hooker: Climatic and environmental changes meant an opening up of their forest habitat in mid to high latitudes, which meant changes in feeding strategy: eating tougher leaves, in particular grass. Specializing in eating leaves involves long gut residence time with the help of bacteria to break down the cellulose, and this is most easily accomplished by evolving large body size.

Halls: What would be your dream discovery, when it comes to very ancient relatives of the horse?

Dr. Hooker: I'm not sure. Science is a bit like a giant jigsaw puzzle. Occasionally if you are lucky you find a piece that links big previously isolated parts of the puzzle. This might be a particularly complete specimen that was previously only known from fragments, thus clarifying relationships, or it might be a new type from a completely new area or time period.

Pliohippus: The More Horse

Gazing into the face of *Pliohippus* was more like looking at the modern horse than any other of its ancient relatives. Its head and neck were longer and its eyes were set wider apart. This gave *Pliohippus* the ability to see both in front and behind itself, making it easier for the horse to detect and escape from predators.

After careful study, scientists discovered *Pliohippus* had deep indentations, called facial fossae, under the eye sockets. That tiny change may have made it possible for *Pliohippus* to expand its vocalizations when communicating with others in the herd.

Pliohippus was the first horse to have a single hoof. Its other toes had evolved into stubs that are still visible on modern horses today. It had a stiff, upright mane and a single stripe down the center of its back. It stood about four feet (twelve hands) high.

Common to the American Great Plains and Canada, *Pliohippus* lived between twelve and six million years ago.

© Mark Hallett

Pliohippus

EQUUS: THE MODERN HORSE

Equus, the modern horse, evolved wild and unbridled in North America about five million years ago. From North America *Equus* migrated to other parts of the world. In fact, fossilized evidence of *Equus* has been found on every continent except Antarctica and Australia.

Unfortunately, a combination of elements, including climate change and over-hunting by early man, drove the American *Equus* population into extinction between ten and eleven thousand years ago. They were reintroduced in South America by Spanish explorers and eventually found their way back North. But the evolutionary links unique to North America were lost forever.

The same fate eventually befell almost all other branches of the wild or native horse family tree. Some scientists, including Dr. Kathleen Hunt, believe only one species of horse within the *Equus* family tree survived—*Equus caballus,* which became the modern domesticated horse. Others say

a second horse, *Equus przewalski*, survived in the Asian wilderness until the twentieth century. Some scientists believe three or four others held on in Europe until they went extinct in the late 1800s. We'll explore each of these possibilities.

Almost all experts agree, three kinds of asses and three types of zebras also survived extinction and still live in the wild. We'll get to know them in the next few chapters.

Most of *Equus* vanished from the continents and territories they once thrived on. But other horses—reintroduced by scientists or released by mankind accidentally—have taken their place.

Equus

Where to See Ancient Horses Today

Aching for a fossil field trip? These North American stops are among the best in the world, when it comes to prehistoric horses. So mark your maps and load up the car. It's time for an ancient horse expedition.

Ashfall Fossil Beds State Historical Park
86930 517th Avenue
Royal, NE 68773

Five different species of prehistoric horse are represented at this amazing park in northeastern Nebraska, famous for the dramatic story behind the mass death and fossilization of hundreds of ancient animals.

Big Bone Lick State Park
3380 Beaver Road
Union, Kentucky 41091

Thanks to the Discovery Trail and the Outdoor Museum, you can experience the fossils of prehistoric horses, mammoths, mastodons, bison and other ancient mammals exactly as they were found at this Kentucky site once visited by Benjamin Franklin and President Thomas Jefferson (not only a president, but an amateur paleontologist).

Hagerman Fossil Beds
National Monument
P.O. Box 570
Hagerman, ID 83332

Hagerman Fossil Beds National Monument contains one of the world's richest known deposits of fossil horses, *Equus simplicidens*, thought to be a link between prehistoric and modern horses. In 1988, the Hagerman horse became Idaho's state fossil and Hagerman Fossil Beds became a national monument. The

Hagerman Fossil Beds

monument contains the Hagerman Horse Quarry, a national natural landmark, recognized as one of the six most important sites in the world when it comes to the fossilized history of the early horse.

John Day Fossil Beds
National Monument
Thomas Condon Paleontology Center
32651 Highway 19
Kimberly, OR 97848

Of special interest is the Turtle Cove Formation Exhibit, but every diorama is exceptional. It's a great chance to explore prehistoric horses and the animals that shared their world.

Page Museum at the
Rancho La Brea Tar Pits
5801 Wilshire Boulevard
Los Angeles, CA. 90036

Over two hundred specimens of the prehistoric Western Horse, or *Equus occidentalis* were trapped in the sticky natural asphalt that has made the La Brea Tar Pits famous for generations. Paleontologists believe this group of *Equus* resembled the modern zebra.

HORSES OF THE WORLD

Scientists group organisms according to a classification system called taxonomy. Horses, zebras, and asses are all members of the Equidae family.

Just like your own family, members of the Equidae family have many similarities. All Equids are mammals, which means that they have hair, nurse their young, and have four-chambered hearts. Additionally, Equids all belong to the order Perissodactyla, a group of mammals called odd-toed ungulates—a scientific term for a mammal with hoofs.

Within the family Equidae, there is one genus and eight species. There are also several subspecies. When scientists are referring to a specific living thing, they use the genus, species, and subspecies to give it a scientific name.

How to Spot an Ungulate

Ungulate comes from the Latin word *unguis* which means nail, claw, or hoof. Today we have odd-toed ungulates and even-toed ungulates. Horses are odd-toed ungulates because they have one hoof on each foot. Below are just a few examples of odd-toed and even-toed ungulates.

ODD-TOED UNGULATES (Perissodactyla)	EVEN-TOED UNGULATES (Cetartiodactyla)
horse	camel
tapir	cattle
rhinoceros	goat

The development of hooves was an important evolutionary step that enabled horses to run faster than their predators. As horses began to evolve, in time only their hooves touched the ground. Eventually the rest of their foot became part of the leg, causing their legs to become longer, increasing the number of joints that move their legs. If you are runner, you know that one way to increase your stride is to run on your toes. It also helps to have long legs.

TAXONOMY OF THE HORSE

KINGDOM:
Animalia

PHYLUM:
Chordata

CLASS:
Mammalia

ORDER:
Perissodactyla

FAMILY:
Equidae

GENUS:
Equus

Domesticated horse
(*Equus caballus*)

Przewalski horse
(*Equus przewalskii*)

Plains zebra
(*Equus quagga*)

Grevy's zebra
(*Equus grevyi*)

Mountain zebra
(*Equus zebra*)

Burro
(*Equus asinus*)

Onager
(*Equus hemionus*)

Kiang
(*Equus kiang*)

WILD HORSES OF EASTERN EUROPE AND ASIA

Over time, the horse evolved into a more powerful animal with strong muscles and a single toe or hoof, enabling some to make the long journey to Asia successfully. Many scientists believe that horses began to migrate from North America to Asia across the Bering Strait land bridge about ten million years ago. Pressure from hunters and competition from other species, along with climatic and botanical changes, made it difficult for the horse population to survive in North America. The land bridge made it possible for some of the horses in North America to escape extinction.

As horses migrated from North America to Asia, they continued on to other parts of the world as well. Some of the migrating horses eventually made Asia and eastern Europe their home. One of these horses holds the very special distinction of being the last species of "wild" horse in the world.

Przewalski horse   Kiang   Onager

THE "WILD" PRZEWALSKI

Many horses around the world are called "wild" and live fierce and rugged lives without the help of humans. But almost all of them are domesticated or tamed horses released by humans, on accident or on purpose. Only one truly "wild" horse still roams its natural habitat in East Asia—the Przewalski.

Equus przewalskii, is also known as the Przewalski horse. In Mongolia, it's called the Takhi, which means "spiritual" in Mongolian. Strong and sturdy, the small (four feet or thirteen hands) horse is known for its distinctive appearance, which is similar to *Pliohippus*. Przewalski has a square, blunt face, stocky body, and short legs. The reddish-brown coat fades to a lighter-toned belly. The dark line down the Przewalski's back is called an eel stripe. Its legs are also sometimes striped, pointing back to its genetic connection to the zebra.

The Przewalski's mane and tail are black, like the stripe down its spine. But the mane stands straight up, even when it's not cut or groomed. No forelock falls between the Przewalski's ears onto its forehead, as is common to domestic horses. And its tail is often unique. The dock-hairs of many Przewalskis are closer to the rear of the horse and can be short and lighter in color. Przewalski's long, flowing tail hair typically doesn't begin until several inches down.

In the wild, Przewalski horses live in herds or family groups, called harems, with one dominant stallion, several mares and their foals, and a number of bachelor males who live under the rule of the stallion. They mark their territories with dung piles and defend their family members even more ferociously than they defend their land.

From Discovery To The Edge Of Extinction

Though they were named in 1881 for Russian explorer Colonel Nikolai M. Przhevalsky (spelled Przewalski in Polish) after he found them in Mongolia in 1879, Przewalski horses were native to Asia long before they were discovered. In fact, images resembling the Przewalski horse have become iconic in prehistoric art etched, painted, or sculpted at dozens of archaeological sites in Asia and eastern Europe.

In most cases, early humans drew or carved dramatic scenes of horses and other regional animals as prey to be hunted—as a food source—rather than as trusted companions. That artwork coupled with fossil evidence including spear tips lodged in ancient horse bones suggest hunting, along with climate changes, made some wild horses vanish. What saved the Przewalski horse from extinction? The same thing that helped drive it so close to the edge: humans.

According to the Museum of Hippology in the Czech Republic, fifty-four Przewalski horses were captured in Mongolia between 1889 and 1903. They were sent to protected locations all over Europe to encourage their odds of reproducing. But only thirteen survived to become the tiny breeding pool for every true Przewalski horse alive today.

Four nations fought to save the sturdy little horse before World War II—Czechoslovakia, Germany, Mongolia, and Ukraine. The Ukrainian herd in Askania Nova was slaughtered by Nazi soldiers. The Mongolian herds, known for centuries as Takhi, dwindled due to a combination of factors, including hunting and habitat destruction.

The last known Przewalski in the wild—a mare known in scientific circles as 231 Orlitza III—was captured in 1947 in Mongolia. Though

The tomb of explorer Nikolai Przhevalsky.

a small herd was allegedly spotted in the Mongolian desert in 1968, they were believed to be extinct in their natural habitats after the mare's capture. So it was up to scientists in Czechoslovakia and Germany to try to save the species.

Other zoos and wildlife sanctuaries joined in the effort to save the Przewalski horse, including the San Diego Zoo and even the Askania Nova region of Ukraine, where one of the last herds was lost during World War II. Thanks to careful captive breeding, the Przewalski population started to grow.

More than 231 foals came out of the zoo in Prague. With numbers on the rise and several herds safely harbored, the first international conference on protecting the species was held in Prague in 1959. The zoo in Prague was charged with continuing the *General Stud Book of the Przewalski Horse*, a careful genetic record of all Przewalski foals born in captivity.

More than 4,650 horses from 1899 to the present are documented in that volume. But according to the zoo in Prague, less than 1,900 are alive today. The Foundation for the Preservation and Protection of the Przewalski Horse says the number is even lower, with roughly 1,435 on record. Only three hundred of those live in the wild.

Bringing the Przewalski back to nature has proved a little more challenging than raising them in zoos, but the effort continues.

The face of the Przewalski horse has a very distinctive shape.

The Przewalski Today

Hoping to see this equestrian maverick with your own two eyes? Consider one of these zoological parks or wildlife preserves for your next family vacation stop and you won't be disappointed. And remember, this is a partial list. More Przewalski horses may be on exhibit near you, so contact your local zoo or wildlife sanctuary for more information.

Wildlife Preserves

Khustain Nuruu National Park—*Mongolia*

Askania Nova—*Ukraine*

Wormwood Forest—*Ukraine (Chernobyl)*

Hortobagy puszta—*Hungary*

The Wilds Wildlife Preserve—*U.S. (Ohio)*

Hustai National Park—*Mongolia*

Cricket St Thomas Wildlife Park—*U.K. (Somerset)*

Zoological Parks

Zoo Praha—*Czech Republic*

Monarto Zoological Park—*Australia*

Western Plains Zoo—*Australia (Sydney)*

Clocaenog Forest—*U.K.*

Whipsnade Wild Animal Park—*U.K.*

Toronto Metropolitan Zoo—*Canada (Toronto)*

Der Zoo der Stadt Munchen—*Germany*

San Diego Zoo—*U.S. (California)*

Minnesota Zoo—*U.S.*

West Midland Safari Park—*U.K.*

Zoo Koln—*Germany*

Kamloops Wildlife Park—*Canada (British Columbia)*

Calgary Zoo—*Canada (Calgary)*

Highland Wildlife Park— *Scotland*

Vienna Zoo—*Austria*

OUT OF THE ASHES

One thriving colony of Przewalski horses roams the site of the world's most devastating nuclear disasters near Pripyat, Ukraine, as if reclaiming their place in history.

On April 26, 1986, an explosion in the Chernobyl nuclear power plant sent a cloud of radioactive dust and destruction over the Western Soviet Union, much of Europe, and even parts of North America. Though only fifty-six human deaths were directly attributed to the accident, over nine thousand people were exposed to enough radiation to lead them to serious health problems during the course of their natural lives.

The area on and near the explosion site—an eighteen-mile radius known as the Zone of

Przewalski horses walk near the Chernobyl nuclear power plant.

Alienation—was so contaminated by radiation it was abandoned by almost all its human population. The air, soil, water, plants, and even the livestock were considered lost causes. Today, they are still guarded by soldiers and police to prevent the spread of radiation.

Animals living within the zone during the disaster were also struck down—either immediately, or within short periods of time, often due to damaged thyroid glands. Those animals that did survive stopped reproducing. Then a strange thing happened. The Przewalski horse helped to turn the tide.

A herd of Przewalski horses had been maintained and strengthened on the Askania Nova wildlife reserve in southern Ukraine for many years. But their human caregivers kept searching for new territories to share with the endangered species. Once the area around Chernobyl was deserted, they wondered how the Przewalski might do in this no-man's land.

In 1998, in spite of radiation concerns, seventeen Przewalski horses from Askania Nova were released into the Chernobyl Zone of Alienation. And to the delight and perhaps surprise of eastern European biologists and zoologists, the herd found a way to survive. In fact, it expanded to a population of twenty-one.

Experts from the National Academy of Sciences of Ukraine carefully examined the herd in 2004 and found they were in good health, including their reproductive systems. Somehow, their migratory habits had helped protect them from radiation and related health problems.

The final report said the success of the herd was a powerful argument for "the use of Przewalski horses in the re-naturalization of ecological disaster areas." In other words, given the chance, wild horses saved by humans could help correct even the most disastrous errors of humankind.

Chernobyl Through Expert Eyes

Mankind couldn't survive near Chernobyl's nuclear ground zero. But the Przewalski horse found a way. How was that possible? According to Dr. Kateryna Slivinska of the Schmalhausen Institute of Zoology in Kyiv, Ukraine, it may be a matter of evolution—simply adapting to survive.

Halls: When were the horses near Chernobyl examined?

Dr. Slivinska: They were examined in February of 2004, because during this season the animals are hungry. We took oats with us to convince them to come as close as possible for examination—as close as possible for wild horses.

Halls: How have the horses thrived in a radioactive region? Why doesn't eating contaminated food and drinking contaminated water hurt them?

Dr. Slivinska: It's only been ten years since these horses were introduced into the Chernobyl Exclusion Zone (another name for the Zone of Alienation). We've established a primary positive fact, that the horses were able to adapt, based on population growth and some parasitic examinations. More studies will follow based on their organic adaptation.

Halls: What does this success mean to Ukraine and to humans?

Dr. Slivinska: That is a philosophical question. But as a scientist, I can answer that horses and other animals can manage even this harsh environment, again, because they adapt. The horse is the dominant species when it comes to the ecosystem of the pasture, in the absence of anthropogenic factors, which means the influence of human beings. Horses survive as their wild ancestors existed. They simply find a way.

The Przewalski horse has thrived in the Chernobyl Exclusion Zone.

THE KIANG: THE ASIAN ASS

Say the words "wild horses" and a certain picture forms in the heads of listeners. But in technical terms, a number of asses also belong in that wild family, including the largest species, Asia's native kiang.

According to the San Diego Zoo, kiangs are especially hardy because of the harshness of their natural habitat. In the high altitude wilds of the Tibetan plateau, temperatures can drop as low as -22°F and precipitation can be as rare as warmth. So kiangs eat as much as they can during the two-to-three-month Tibetan growing season. They pack on the calories and fat in order to survive the brutal winters.

Kiangs have tough mouths with thick lips so they can graze on grasses, shrubs, or weeds.

For centuries, the kiang or *Equus kiang,* thrived from as far north as Mongolia to many regions of the Middle East. Today, they are an endangered species on conservation lists all over the world. The kiangs exist in China, Tibet, and northern India.

Inside the Heavenly Horse Tomb

More than 11,500 artifacts were found in the royal Cheonmachong Tomb in Tumuli Park, South Korea. But the Cheonmado, a flying horse painted on the skin of an ancient white birch, was the only painted image ever discovered in the park's twenty-three grassy mound tombs. Created during the late 5th century BC, and known as the Korean Pegasus, the painting and other artifacts proved how important horses were in ancient South Korea.

ONAGER: THE PERSIAN WILD ASS

The onager (*Equus hemionus*) is also referred to as the Persian wild ass. It stands about four feet (twelve hands) high and has a small, slender body. The Onager has a white stomach and brown legs, along with a characteristic black spinal stripe on each side of its back.

If you ever come across a wild ass, you will easily be able to tell it apart from a horse or a zebra. They are much smaller, with a short, stiff mane, and big ears. Despite rumors to the contrary, they are typically intelligent, with excellent vision and hearing. When confronted by a predator, they are more likely to run than fight. And wow, can they run! Onagers can reach speeds up to forty-five miles per hour. If a predator does manage to corner one, it kicks—hard!

Most onagers live in herds. However, stallions tend to live alone and only join a herd during the summer breeding season. They are often aggressive and fight ferociously with other stallions in the herd.

For thousands of years, onagers were prevalent throughout eastern Europe. Over time, they have been over hunted for their meat, and today they are an endangered species.

WHO FIRST TAMED THE BEASTS?

Asia is the last region to harbor a true wild horse (as compared with a horse that's gone back to the wild after being tamed by humans). But when did domestication begin? Who first tamed horses in the wild?

A study published by Carnegie Museum anthropologist Rosemary Capo and graduate student Andrew Stiff in 2006 suggests it might have been a group of nomadic villagers called the Botai in Kazakhstan, south of China. And the proof is in the poop.

Traces of horse manure more than 5,600 years old found inside a circular space marked by ancient postholes is circumstantial evidence the circle was a corral. And corrals

The Botai made tools with horse bones.

are used for domesticated animals. The Botai must have corralled horses, even as they migrated with each seasonal change.

How did they use their captured horses? According to Carnegie Museum curator of Anthropology Sandra L. Olsen, the Botai depended on horses for almost everything. They used them as pack animals and to ride. They ate horse meat. They used the hides for clothing and the bones for tools and other useful items. They may have even milked the horses to make a protein-rich drink known as koumiss, still enjoyed by their ancestors today.

Nomadic ancestors of the Botai drink koumiss (horse milk).

WILD HORSES OF WESTERN EUROPE

We know prehistoric wild horses migrated to Asia thanks to the Bering Strait land bridge. And we know *Equus przewalskii* is the last undomesticated species of wild horses on the planet. But did the same Asian horse live in western Europe too? The answer is no, according to Carnegie Museum curator of Anthropology Sandra L. Olsen. She believes the European wild horse was *Equus ferus*, though she admits it closely resembled the Asiatic wild horse, *Equus przewalskii*.

According to the International Museum of the Horse, in Lexington, KY, that second wild horse, *Equus ferus*, is also known as the Tarpan. It evolved east of Asia, leaving its mark everywhere it roamed.

Tarpan

Sorraia

Camargue

Konik

PRESERVING THE TARPAN

According to the Oklahoma State University Department of Animal Science, the Tarpans lived wild in Russia, Spain, and France, until the brutal Scythians tamed them in 3000 BC. Known for drinking the blood of the first enemy killed in a tribal battle, the nomadic Scythians were almost completely dependent on the newly domesticated wild horses.

Some experts believe the Tarpan is directly related to modern horses also called Tarpans. But further studies by a team of German scientists from the Institute for Anthropology put that theory in question.

Tarpans have thick winter coats to protect them from the harsh climate.

In 1998, a team of archaeologists from Kazakhstan and France excavated a dramatic Scythian burial ground in the high Altai Mountains of eastern Kazakhstan. For over 2,300 years, the contents of the burial site, including thirteen sacrificed horses, went undetected.

Ghent University scientific researcher Woulter Gheyle, who participated in the dig and subsequent study, said, "The horses were unique. They were found in the frozen part of the tomb, they were not touched by the robbery, and they were very well preserved." So well preserved that DNA could be extracted.

After analyzing the ancient DNA and comparing it to the DNA of six hundred modern horses, genetics experts found they were not bred from one strain of horses, but instead had more diverse backgrounds. That doesn't mean the Tarpan didn't exist. It only means those thirteen horses were not purebred specimens.

What was believed to be the last of the purebred wild Tarpans died in Askania Nova in Ukraine in 1876. Farmers disliked the untamed herds and drove them to extinction; much the way humans are making it impossible for wild horses to survive in the shrinking prairies of the United States.

Conservationists in Europe tried to replicate the look of the prehistoric species by mating horses with Tarpan characteristics. The first attempts took place in Germany in 1933. This mixed breed has been re-introduced and they look very much like their Tarpan ancestors. New herds of the modern Tarpan are being released into the wilds where their ancestors once roamed freely.

SPAIN'S HORSE OF THE SWAMP

Like the Tarpan, the roots of the Iberian Sorraia horse—*Equus stenonius*—are very difficult to trace. But some believe its ancient ancestor, is the Marismeno (which means "horse of the swamp" in its native Spain). According to local legends, the Sorraia is a horse that survived naturally in the wild until civilization drove it to the brink of extinction in the early 1900s.

If not for Italian born Portuguese scientist Dr. Ruy d'Andrade, the rare horse would have vanished, according to *Conquistador Magazine* and the Sorraia Horse Nature Reserve in Alpiarça, Portugal. On a trip to the river Sorraia in Portugal, Dr. d'Andrade discovered and documented a dwindling herd of the dun (pale tan) and grullo (pale gray) colored native horses.

To protect the rare wild horses, he bought a large section of their grazing territory and offered them protection, while allowing them to exist as they would in nature. He admired the small horses, roughly four and one-half feet (fourteen hands) high with markings in sync with ancient breeds, including striping on the legs. He worked to prove they were the ancestors of modern breeds popular today— Andalusian, Lusitano, Friesian, and Lipizzan. Roughly one hundred Sorraia horses exist today in Portugal and Germany, 70 percent on the ranch of José Luís Sommer d'Andrade, the grandson of Ruy d'Andrade. Will they slip into extinction any time soon? "Not while I'm alive," Jose says in an interview on the Sorraia Horse Nature Reserve Web site. But after he's gone, their fate could be uncertain.

For now, the Sorraia horses graze happily in the wilds of Portugal on the d'Andrade ranch and on the nature reserve. If they continue to enjoy special protection, a piece of Iberia's ancient past may also be preserved.

Yet most of their horses were fed a luxurious diet of barley, dates, and camel's milk. Arabian horses became a part of the Bedouin's family, sharing their food and living in their tents. It is not surprising that Arabian horses today have a strong bond with humans.

It is believed that there are five main lines of Arabian horses. Each line was bred by one of the five Bedouin tribes. In order to keep the pedigree pure, the lines were kept separate, and the tribes did not let the horses interbreed. Purebred mares were highly valued by the Bedouins. Stallions were often difficult to manage in the tent communities of the desert. They were also more difficult to control in combat.

If you look at an Arabian horse, you can clearly see the features that the Bedouin tribes valued. These horses were bred for one very specific purpose—battle. Arabian horses needed to have a large lung capacity and strong endurance in order to fight in the harsh desert. Their unique physical characteristics and small stature were selectively bred in order to produce a horse that was strong and fast in an unforgiving environment.

The Anatomy of an Arabian Horse

Arabian horses aren't your average horse.

	Arabian Horses	Other Horses
number of vertebrae	23	24
number of ribs	17	18
number of lumbar bones	5	6
number of tail vertebrae	16	18

SAVING IRAQ'S ARABIAN TREASURE

Arabian horses have been one of the most popular breeds for centuries. Even Iraqi dictator Sadam Hussein championed a herd of one hundred fine Arabian horses when he ruled the country.

When the war began in Iraq, in March of 2003, these innocent animals were caught in the crossfire. Key targets, not far from where the National Arabian Herd was sheltered, were struck hard.

Because of the obvious danger, the herd's caregivers were forced to seek temporary safety. By the time they were able to

U.S. Army Captain William Sumner (left) and a member of the rescue team pose with one of the captured Arabian horses.

return to check on the horses, many had been stolen by looters and other hungry, frightened people.

U.S. Army Captain William Sumner was an archaeologist assigned to help retrieve and archive priceless artifacts once housed at the National Museum of Iraq. But when he heard about the endangered animals, the focus of his mission changed.

"A lot of people were helping the people," Sumner said in the *Charlotte Daily Mail* in May of 2007, "but almost no one was helping the animals." So he took on the challenge of saving war-ravaged animals, including the missing Arabian herd.

After two failed missions and careful negotiations, sixteen of the one hundred Arabian horses were rescued. With donations

from groups like Tack for Iraq, the horses are now safe in their new home at the Baghdad Zoo, which reopened for business on July 20, 2003.

"But more needs to be done," says Earth Organization founder Lawrence Anthony, who also cared for endangered animals in Iraq. "We are lobbying for the U.S. and British armies to form a small task team to look after enclosed wildlife in war zones, so there can never be a repeat of the Baghdad debacle." If kids want to help, Anthony says, "they can join or form Earth Organization chapters. We have an office in

Sixteen of the one hundred Arabian horses were rescued and taken to their new home at the Baghdad Zoo.

the U.S. which can help with this if they are interested." Donations are also welcome at the International Fund for Animal Welfare or the Baghdad Zoo.

Veterinarians check the Arabian horses for injuries after the rescue.

WILD HORSES OF AFRICA

Remember the ungulates? Africa is home to more ungulates than any other continent in the world—over ninety species. Living among the elephants, tapirs, rhinoceros and gazelles are several members of the *Equus* family.

It is unclear if horses were native to Africa and then vanished, as they did on most continents, or were introduced by foreign visitors. What we do know is that five species of horses, the plains zebra, the Grevy's zebra, the mountain zebra, the African ass, and the Namibia horse, still thrive in many regions of Africa today.

Grevy's zebra   Plains zebra   Mountain zebra

Wild ass   Namibia horse

ZEBRAS, ZEBRAS, ZEBRAS

Wild horses, as we've come to imagine them, aren't native to Africa, but another *Equus* family member evolved and thrived on the continent. Zebras—three different, distinctive kinds—are true and authentic wild horses in their own right, even if they took the *Equus* family tree in a new, striped direction.

The plains zebra or *Equus quagga*, also known as Burchell's zebra, is the most common zebra, standing almost four and one-half feet (thirteen hands) high. It lives in the grasslands and savannahs of east Africa. Built more like a stocky pony, this zebra is thick, with shorter legs than its two other African counterparts.

Grevy's zebra, *Equus grevyi*—the largest zebra at almost five feet (fourteen hands) high—was once common to east Africa too. But because of hunting and competition with

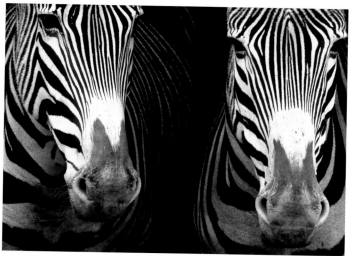

Unlike other zebra species, the Grevy's zebra does not form permanent herds.

local farmers for open land, it's now endangered and limited to game preserves in Kenya. It was named for French President Jules Grevy after the zebra was presented to him as a gift in the late 1800s.

Mountain zebras or *Equus zebra* are about four feet (twelve hands) high and are found

How to Tell a Zebra by Its Stripes

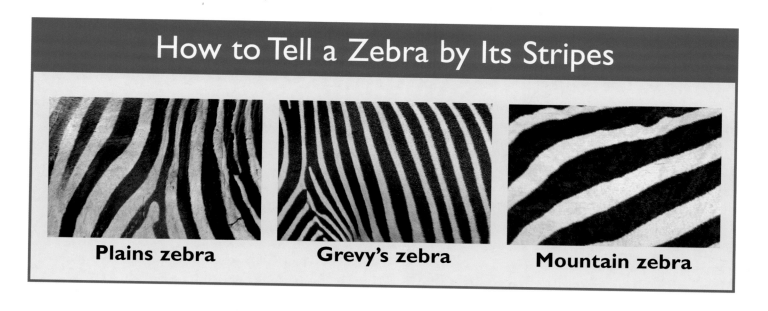

Plains zebra   **Grevy's zebra**   **Mountain zebra**

only in the south and southwestern regions of Africa. They are also endangered. Mountain zebras have sleeker coats than other zebras. One group of mountain zebras has thinner white stripes. The other has thinner black stripes.

Though we tend to see all black and white striped zebras as identical, they are in many ways unique. For example, no two stripe patterns are exactly alike. They are as distinctive, when closely examined, as the human fingerprint. So scientists who study zebras can learn to tell them apart by their stripe patterns and individual scars.

Zebras have excellent vision and hearing. They are swift—able to run up to thirty-five miles per hour. And they have a defensive

Plains zebra stallions fight for a dominant role in the herd.

kick that can leave a predator's head spinning.

They are more successful plant eaters than some other horses, because they will browse

Mountain zebras are skilled climbers and often live in the high elevations of South Africa.

Zebra herds usually have one stallion, one alpha female, and several mares.

and graze, meaning they will eat leaves and grasses, depending on what's available. They are water dependent, like all wild horses, but have evolved to need less water than most of their wild or domesticated relations.

All zebras live in family groups called herds or harems with a stallion, an alpha female, and a number of other mares and their foals. When a mother zebra gives birth, she insists on several days of isolation with the

Zebra Fun Facts

Did you know that zebras

. . . have black skin under their coats?

. . . give birth to babies with brown and white stripes?

. . . sometimes have thin "shadow" stripes between their darker stripes?

. . . take mud baths to get clean? When the mud flakes off, loose hair and shed skin go with it.

. . . wait between twelve and fourteen months to give birth to a new baby?

. . . can begin walking just twenty minutes after they're born?

. . . have night vision as good as a cat or an owl?

. . . communicate with sounds **AND** facial expressions? A smile or bare-teeth greeting is a sign of non-aggression.

new baby, so it will bond to her through sight, scent, and vocalizations. Once the bond has been made, mother and foal rejoin the herd.

Male foals also bond with the stallion, their father, and may stay as growing bachelors for one to four years. But, eventually, the males will either challenge other stallions for mares to start their own harems, or they'll leave to live in bachelor herds—groups of younger males who band together but aren't ready or able to lead harems of their own.

When a harem is challenged by a hungry predator, they form a semi-circle to defend themselves against the meat eater. If one of their own is hurt, they will often circle around the wounded herd member to protect it from harm.

Zebra "Stamp" of Approval

On July 1, 2005, the South African Postal Service issued a page of stamps created by artist Hein Botha based on South African folklore. Among those stories told in tiny squares was the isiZulu legend of how the zebra got its stripes.

IsiZulu (Zulu) is one of eleven national languages spoken in South Africa. More than ten million South African citizens speak it, so its inclusion in the special stamp project was not surprising. This is a retelling of the legend played out.

Long ago, a huge, ferocious baboon decided everything he could survey was his and his alone, including the river water. No one else, Baboon said, was allowed to take even a sip from that day forward.

A proud white zebra stallion named Dube didn't think the rule was fair. He challenged Baboon to a fight to determine who really had a right to drink from the river or live on the land.

Baboon was as fierce as Dube was brave, so the battle was long and brutal. When Baboon managed to cast Dube into a searing fire, the other animals thought all was lost. But the pain of the burning embers nudged Dube forward and gave him the will to fight on.

Dube gathered all the strength he had left and focused it on one powerful kick against Baboon, sending him soaring through the open air. Baboon landed with such force, a bare spot appeared on his hindquarters that can be seen on all baboons to this day. Black stripes from the fire forever changed Dube's once snow-white body. But because he won his battle with Baboon, all zebras now wear the stripes with pride in remembrance of how Dube freed the life-giving waters for every animal.

B5

SOUTH AFRICA

How Zebra got his Stripes

South African Folklore Hein Botha 2005

WILD *EQUUS* COUSIN: THE ASS

In addition to zebras, other members of the horse family at one point thrived on the African continent. Wild asses found a workable niche and definitely made their mark on the region's ancient history.

According to Carnegie Museum curator Sandra L. Olsen today, only one wild ass survives in Africa—the African wild ass. Also known as *Equus africanus*, the African wild ass once lived in Somalia, Ethiopia, Sudan, and Eritrea as two distinct subgroups—the Nubian wild ass and the Somali wild ass. Smart, swift, and sure-footed in the desert flats or rocky African territories, they were so admired by Egyptians that they were domesticated in Egypt six thousand years ago. But the first group is probably gone—all but extinct in the wild, according to the San Diego Zoo. The Somali subgroup—four feet (twelve hands) high with pale gray coats, white bellies, striped legs, and black spiked manes—is critically endangered.

If the Somali wild ass is lost, we lose a wild horse of distinctive behaviors. Where most horses live many daily hours in herds, the wild ass lives a more solitary existence. Stallions seldom interact with the mares in their harems. Instead, they patrol the perimeters of their territories to mark them with their urine and feces, silently saying, "This spot is taken." If that territory is challenged by another stallion, the two will often fight for dominance, in part because many territories include watering holes that are rare and hard to find.

Stallions will also fight for the right to mate with females, who gestate for eleven months before giving birth to a new foal.

Even the mares and foals live alone or in very small herds until the rainy season comes and makes food a little easier to find. During that same rainy season, foals are born and stallions mate with mares to guarantee the species might survive in the coming year. With their habitats shrinking, it remains to be seen whether nature alone can help increase their dwindling numbers and better their odds.

Unlike most wild horses that form herds, the Somali wild ass lives a more solitary existence.

WILD HORSES OF NAMIBIA

How they found their way to the unforgiving climate of the Namib Desert is a mystery, even to historians. They have never been native to the region. But wild horses—over 150 of them—have lived and thrived in South Africa's Namibia for nearly a century. And if local conservationists have their way, they're there to stay.

One theory suggests a load of nineteenth century imported horses was shipwrecked on its way to the Skeleton Coast, not far from the mouth of the Orange River. Only the strongest, most determined horses could have made their way to the desert.

Others suggest that a German breeder living in South Africa was called to service in World War I and never returned. In time, without real ownership, the horses were abandoned and learned how to survive in the wild.

However they came to live in the Namib Desert, wild horses have been cherished but controversial immigrants ever since. Wild horse fans lobby to feed and water the horses in times of drought. Those who feel the outsiders should be removed from the Namib Desert worry that the horses will upset the natural ecologic balance. Because the desert is home to rare plants and animals native to the region, some locals fear life with foreign horses will push those species toward extinction.

AFRICA: ROCK ART OF THE SAN

For more than seventy thousand years, natives of South Africa marked their rituals in stone petroglyphs. Over fifty thousand examples dot the landscape of Southern Africa, many created by the people known as the San. And wild horses—likely zebras or asses—were sometimes depicted.

For centuries, scientists who studied the ways of the San saw these paintings as something simple, like a menu of what the locals liked to hunt and eat. But these vivid illustrations—alive with the colors of red, orange, yellow, black, and white created by mixing clay, burnt wood, ochre oxide and even animal blood—revealed much more than dietary preferences.

Because a German language expert named Wilhelm Bleek and his sister-in-law, Lucky Lloyd, carefully collected and translated twelve thousand pages of San folklore and ritual practices in the late nineteeth century, anthropologists finally made the

The horse in the rock art (above) resembles a zebra.

connection. Many of the rock art paintings were spiritual in nature.

San holy men believed animals had an invisible power—a supernatural energy they would need to cure illness within their tribes or to bring relief from a drought. So they honored the animals both in rituals and in skillfully crafted rock wall art pieces.

That connection was made when scientists combined what they learned in the twelve thousand translated pages with what they saw at Game Pass, a natural shelter of sandstone in the Drakensberg Mountains. Spectacular rock art at that location helped make sense of the deeper meaning behind the San images.

Another site, the Sevilla Rock Art Trail in the Clanwilliam region of South Africa's Western Cape, features nine different rock art panels, including one that features a San villager with bow and arrow closely following what seems to be a wild horse.

Not every work of rock art—called kukummi by the San—was connected to a spiritual ritual or desire. Some were like news announcements or entertaining stories. But the San believed that the inspiration for each kukummi "floated in from afar."

Tragically, an enemy tribe wiped out the San. South African author Peter Slingsby, who has documented the San story and rock art in fiction for young readers and nonfiction travel guidebooks for adults, believes the images are a national treasure, but voices a protective

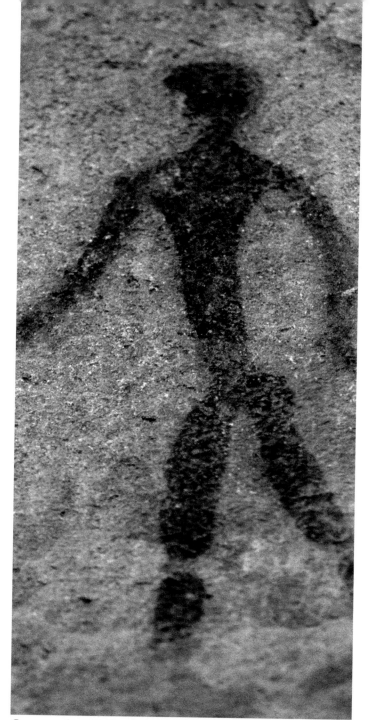

San rock art depicts prehistoric life in Africa.

statement. "When we look at the fading images which the San have left behind," Slingsby has written, "we are humbled by the terrible fate which overtook these artists and their descendants. We should take special care to admire and preserve their legacy."

WILD HORSES OF THE AMERICAS

As we learned earlier, the history of the horse started on the North American continent. From the tiny prehistoric *Hyracotherium* to the modern day domesticated breeds, wild horses are rooted there. They continued to thrive until they were lost to extinction roughly ten thousand years ago. Thankfully, explorers brought domesticated horses back to the Americas centuries later.

Those feral horses, imported from foreign continents but related by blood to the ancients, became America's new breed of wild horses. In North America, wild horses can be found in ten western states, in remote regions of Canada, the Bahamas, and on several barrier islands off the Atlantic Coast. As time went on, these horses were given many exotoic names, like the Chincoteague ponies of Virginia and Maryland, the Abaco Barbs of the Bahamas, and the ponies of Assateague on the Barrier Islands. But most are known collectively as wild mustangs.

Mustang   Abaco Barb   Burro

WILD MUSTANGS OF NORTH AND SOUTH AMERICA

Feral or wild horses in North America are often called mustangs. But what does "mustang" mean and where did the word come from? According to the Oklahoma State University department of animal science, the word mustang comes from the Spanish word *mesteno*, meaning "stray" or "feral animal." The Spanish word came from the Latin term *animalia mixta*, meaning "mixed beast."

Unlike most mammals, horses live in year-round bands, composed of several stallions and a harem of females. Researchers have found that some stallions and their harems have been together for many years. Males often battle one another for control of a harem. It is not uncommon for a stallion to bite the leg tendons of an opponent in combat. Once the tendon has been severed, the winning male takes control of the harem.

Today, there are hundreds of wild horse herds in North America. Their numbers are estimated to be about fifteen thousand in total, whereas once vast herds of millions roamed western North America. Even though horses produce just one foal per year, herds can expand 17 percent per year. The vast majority of wild horses are in Nevada, with a fair

Mustangs are mixed breed horses that come in many colors and sizes.

number spreading throughout the west in Wyoming, Colorado, and Oregon—states where there is a lot of public land. Another herd of note roams the Barrier Islands off the coast of North Carolina.

Though horses went extinct in the Americas ten thousand years ago, even as they began to thrive in Europe and other continents almost worldwide, they were reintroduced when Spanish explorers landed in South America.

Sixteenth century Conquistador Don Pedro Mendoza imported warhorses to help conquer Argentina. Horses that escaped the warriors from Spain—or the native people they were trying to vanquish—reclaimed the American wilds their ancestors had once galloped.

From the bloodlines of those proud, ancient warhorses came the Criollo, the

Wild mustangs roam freely throughout South America.

South American mustangs are decendants of Spanish warhorses.

Barb and the Andalusian, along with other South American breeds. Natural selection—the survival of strong horses and the demise of horses too weak to endure—made South America's mustang horses strong and tough.

For four centuries, the descendants of Spanish horses fought to survive in the new world. Over time, Native Americans and newer immigrants hunted for and tamed the sturdy animals as companions and help-mates, not food. But deep in their DNA, these wild horses are Spanish warriors with a hearty will to survive.

ABACO BARB

Just 150 miles off the coast of Florida lives a mysterious herd of wild horses called Abaco Barbs. Their ancestors were originally from the Barbary Coast of North Africa, but they were taken to Spain and Portugal after the fall of the Roman Empire.

The horses arrived on Abaco Island in the early 1500s. Many believe that they are the survivors of Spanish shipwrecks. In 2002, the Horse of the America's Registry designated the wild horses of Abaco as a new strain of the critically endangered Spanish Barb breed. Because the horses have been isolated on Abaco Island for hundreds of years, scientists believe that the Abaco Barb represents the purest strain of the breed in existence.

At one time, hundreds of these wild horses raced across Abaco Island. During the 1960s, most of the herd was slaughtered by humans who thought the horses were a nuisance. Only three of these beautiful horses managed to survive. The remaining Barbs were placed in protective captivity and eventually increased the herd to twelve.

The mystery of the Abaco Barbs is far from being solved, and time is running out. In 2005 two died of lung disease, and there have not been any foals born since 1998. Without the funding for research and medical care, the wild horses of Abaco may not survive. Today, only eight Abaco Barbs are left to run free on Abaco Island.

WILD BURROS

Along with the horse, the Spanish also brought donkeys, called "burros" in Spanish, to North America beginning around the 1500s. The ancestors of the modern burro, *Equus asinus*, are the Nubian and Somalian subspecies of the African wild ass. In fact, new research done in Egypt shows that the only anatomical signs of the transition from ass to burro are changes in the metatarsal bone of the lower leg. The burro's leg is more compact, which indicates that the burro may have evolved to adapt to the heavy loads that they have carried throughout history.

During the U.S. gold rush, the strong, hard working burro became popular with miners and gold prospectors. Sure footing, plus the ability to withstand high temperatures and carry heavy loads, made burros a great asset to the miners as they trekked long distances across the deserts in search of gold and silver. As the West became more heavily populated, many of these burros were no longer needed, and they were turned loose into the desert. The wild burros of the West are direct descendents of the animals that ran away or were abandoned.

It is common for burros and horses to interbreed, but their offspring are usually unable to reproduce. A mule is the offspring of a jack and a female horse. The mating of a male horse and a female burro produces a hinny.

A male burro is called a jack, and the female is called a jenny. Female wild burros can give birth to one colt each year, which grows to an average weight of about 350 pounds.

Since the wild burro has no natural predator, most young burros reach maturity and live as long as twenty-five years in the wild. It is estimated that there are about three thousand wild burros in the United States today.

Wild Horses in Today's North America

Would you like to see wild horses in North America? Many sanctuaries exist all over the country. A few are listed below, and you can contact the United States Department of the Interior's Bureau of Land Management for a more extensive list. If you can't make your way to their pastures, you can write for more information to get to know these proud steeds a little better.

U.S. Department of the Interior
Bureau of Land Management
Office of Public Affairs
1849 C Street, Room 406-LS
Washington, DC 20240

The Wild Free-Roaming Horses and Burros Act of 1971 was designed to manage and protect bands of wild horses across the U.S on federal lands. Those protections have eroded as the numbers of horses have grown. But the BLM does provide some assistance to the animals, as well as handling an adoption program that allows qualified Americans to adopt healthy horses and burros. Unfortunately, the round-up of these adoption animals often causes injuries that endanger wild horses, especially foals and pregnant mares. But

wild horse fans are hoping the government will enact new laws in the future to better care for the animals.

Assateague Island
7307 Stephen Decatur Highway
Berlin, MD 21811

Popular folklore says these lovely wild horses are descendents of horses that survived a historic shipwreck by swimming to the island. No official records confirm such a disaster. According to the National Park Service, it's more likely the horses were brought to the island by their seventeenth century owners to help them avoid paying livestock taxes. Either way, they've successfully adapted to living on the stormy islands and are a wonder to see.

Chincoteague National Wildlife Refuge
PO Box 62
Chincoteague Island, VA 23336

Approximately 150 Chincoteague ponies—two separate herds—are safely harbored in this refuge, once owned by the local volunteer fire department. Every July, both herds are rounded up during the Annual Pony Penning and Auction, and a few of the foals and yearlings are sold to benefit the local emergency services, including fire and ambulance service.

The wild horses of Assateague Island.

Wild Horses of Shackleford Banks
FSH, Inc.
306 Golden Farm Road
Beaufort, NC 28516

Called "Banker ponies" because they are small horses that linger near the banks of these North Carolina islands, the wild horse of Shackleford Banks are the descendents of sixteenth century horses from Hispaniola (a region between Cuba and Puerto Rico). Cared for by a foundation, they are considered a valuable historic asset.

Wild Horse Island
490 North Meridian
Kalispell, MT 59901

Centuries ago, Salish-Kootenai Indians allegedly pastured their horses on Wild Horse Island to protect them from being stolen by members of other Indian nations. Today, the horses are part of a protected natural environment and historic preserve on Flathead Lake in Montana.

Pryor Mountain Wild Horse Refuge
Bighorn Canyon National Recreation
Area Visitor Center
PO Box 487
Lovell, WY 82431

As part of the migratory Spanish horse groups that moved from South America into the southwestern U.S., the horses of Pryor Mountain have a rich and lengthy American history. Protected by the Wyoming State legislature, these classic American mustangs are safe, at least for now. You can see them near the Bighorn Canyon National Recreation area.

Chilcotin Wild Horse Sanctuary
1010 Foul Bay Rd.
Victoria, BC Canada V8S 4J1

Though wild horses enjoy some protections in the United States, in Canada they are not always so lucky. British Columbia's Chilcotin sanctuary may soon be one of the rare exceptions. Cherished by the region's Xeni Gwe'tin First Nations, a tribal nation native to the area, the horses are considered valuable and sacred. But they are in danger until concerned citizens are granted their wish for a full-fledged sanctuary.

LET THE RESCUE BEGIN

In each section of this book we've explored wild horses, past and present, natural and reintroduced, on almost every continent around the globe. We'll bring our exploration to a close by discussing how to protect the remaining wild horses from the same fate that befell their ancestors.

In most cases, humans drove ancient wild horses to extinction, mostly in a quest for food. We no longer hunt horses for meat and clothing in most nations. But as human beings develop and move onto more and more open land, wild horses face a future as potentially dire as that of their ancestors.

The Bureau of Land Management protects wild horses on U.S. federal land.

Many of us love and respect all kinds of horses. But they won't be safe unless we fight to make it so. Laws written by senators and congressmen within the United States government change as different people are elected to office. If enough representatives respect the wild horse, the laws will offer them protection. If they don't, thousands of wild horses face a brutal and painful death sentence.

Unless we learn to coexist with the wildlife which helped establish the fragile ecological balance making life possible for people, wild horses may vanish again—this time slaughtered as a matter of convenience, rather than to ensure human survival.

Abaco Wild Horse Fund, Inc.

The Abaco Barb is considered to be the most endangered horse in the world. The Abaco Wild Horse Fund was founded by Milanne Rehor to provide these rare and beautiful horses with a safe and secure future by educating the public about the inappropriate human intervention that has prevented them from once again reaching viable numbers. Today, only eight Abaco horses survive.

Arkwild, Inc.
2829 Bird Ave.
Ste. 5, PMB #170
Miami, FL 33133

American Mustang and Burro Association

The American Mustang and Burro Association works to educate people about the plight of our country's living legends of the American West—wild horses and burros. They offer advice and support to adopters of wild horses and maintain a registry of wild equine and their descendents.

American Mustang and Burro Association
PO Box 1013
Grass Valley, CA 95945

Black Hills Wild Horse Sanctuary

Over five hundred wild horses from state governments, Bureau of Land Management and Forest Service land make their home on eleven thousand acres in the pristine Black Hills of South Dakota. The wild horse herds graze on prairie grasses and water from the Cheyenne River. The Black Hills Wild Horse Sanctuary is founded by Dayton O. Hyde.

Black Hills Wild Horse Sanctuary
PO Box 998
Hot Springs, SD 57757

BLM National Wild Horse and Burro Program

The Bureau of Land Management (BLM) protects, manages, and controls wild horses and burros under the authority of the Wild Free-Roaming Horses and Burros Act of 1971 to ensure that herds thrive on healthy rangelands. The BLM manages these living symbols of the Western spirit as part of its multiple-use mission under the 1976 Federal Land Policy and Management Act.

BLM National Wild Horse and Burro Program
Office of Public Affairs
1849 C Street, Room 406-LS
Washington, DC 20240

Corolla Wild Horse Fund

The Corolla Wild Horse Fund was formed in 1989 by a group of concerned citizens to heighten awareness about the presence of wild horses that live along the Outer Banks of North Carolina.

Corolla Wild Horse Fund
PO Box 361
Corolla, NC 27927

Florida Wild Horse and Burro Association, Inc.

The Florida Wild Horse and Burro Association's mission is to develop and carry out educational and mentoring programs for Floridians who have adopted horses and burros from the Bureau of Land Management. They work to promote successful adoptions, provide pre-adoption information, support, and assist new adopters and owners of BLM horses and burros and through a statewide network of members.

Florida Wild Horse and Burro Association, Inc.
P.O. Box 481
Fountain, FL 32438

Lifesavers, Inc.

Lifesavers works to prevent mustangs from suffering abuse, neglect and slaughter. Lifesavers rescues unwanted and discarded mustangs, rehabilitates and trains them, if necessary, and places them into new loving homes with adopters who will make a life commitment to care for the horse; provides sanctuary for crippled and aged mustangs for the lives of the horses; and aims to educate the public on wild horse issues and promote the image of the mustang.

Lifesavers, Inc.
23809 East Avenue J
Lancaster, California 93535

Mustang and Wild Horse Rescue of Georgia

This organization promotes the adoption of mustangs by counseling and training those considering adopting or caring for a horse. They are dedicated to the rescue and rehabilitation of BLM mustangs and wild horses.

Mustang and Wild Horse Rescue of Georgia
786 Four Mile Church Rd.
Ball Ground, GA 30107

National Wild Horse Association

The NWHA was established in 1971 when Congress passed the Wild, Free-Roaming Horse and Burro Act with one important purpose in mind—ensuring the welfare of wild horses and burros and their survival in an ecologically balanced environment on the open range.

National Wild Horse Association
P.O. Box 12207
Las Vegas, NV 89112

The Nokota Horse Conservancy

The Nokota Horse Conservancy is a nonprofit organization established in 1999 to preserve the unique and historical Nokota horse. These wild horses of the northern plains inhabited the Little Missouri badlands, now encompassed by Theodore Roosevelt National Park, for more than a century. They were removed by the National Park Service and sold during the 1980s and 1990s. The vast majority of the remaining Nokota horses now survive on the overburdened Kuntz Ranch. The goals of the Nokota Horse Conservancy are to preserve these important horses by caring for them, promoting awareness of their plight, value, and use to others, and by working to establish a sanctuary where they can survive into the future.

The Nokota Horse Conservancy
420 S. Broadway
Linton, ND 58552

Return to Freedom
American Wild Horse Sanctuary

The sanctuary's mission is to provide a safe haven for herds of wild horses and burros that are in danger of being separated, slaughtered, abused, or left to starve to death. Currently home for around two hundred horses including some very rare breeds, the sanctuary focuses on many key "horse issues" including education, preservation of natural habitat, and changing of legislation. One of the horses at the sanctuary was rescued off the floor of a slaughterhouse after a U.S. federal court ruling saved her life!

Return to Freedom American Wild Horse Sanctuary
PO Box 926
Lompoc, CA 93438

Wild Horse Sanctuary

Rather than allow eighty wild horses living on public land to be destroyed, the founders of the Wild Horse Sanctuary made a decision to rescue these unwanted horses and create a safe home for them.

Wild Horse Sanctuary
PO Box 30
Shingletown, CA 96088

Wild Horse Spirit Ltd.

Since 1993, Wild Horse Spirit has provided a sanctuary for free-roaming wild horses that have been abused or neglected on public and private lands.

Wild Horse Spirit Ltd.
25 Lewers Creek Road
Carson City, NV 89704

Wild Horses of Shackleford Banks

Sometimes called Banker ponies, the Shackleford horses live along the Outer Banks of North Carolina. The foundation was put into place to help protect the horse's natural habitat and create a registry to maintain records of the individual horses.

Wild Horses of Shackleford Banks
306 Golden Farm Road
Beaufort, NC 28516

Foundation for the Preservation and Protection of the Przewalski Horse

Founded in 1977, when there were only three hundred Przewalksi horses in the world, the Foundation for the Preservation and Protection of the Przewalski Horse had two missions: the development and implementation of a computerized studbook information system and re-release of the species into its original habitat. In 1992, the first shipment of Przewalski horses to Mongolia took place. With those two goals a reality, the foundation has since worked as advocates for the protection of the Przewalski horse as well as encouraged research on the last surviving wild horse.

Foundation for the Preservation and Protection
of the Przewalski Horse
Boomdijk 43
3286 LD Klaaswaal
The Netherlands

BIBLIOGRAPHY

INTERVIEWS

December 2006
Staab, Gary; sculptor/owner Staab Studios.

January 2007
Hooker, Jerry Ph.D; Paleontologist, National History Museum, London, England.

April 2007
Shecter, Vicky Alvear; author, "Alexander the Great Rocks the World."

May 2007
Slivinska, Kateryna, Ph.D; Geneticist, Department of Parasitology, Schmalhausen Institute of Zoology, Kyiv, Ukraine.

June 2007
Anthony, Lawrence; Thula Thula Game Reserve, author. June 23, 2007

Bahn, Paul, Ph.D; archaeologist and author, international rock art authority. June 22, 2007

Clemons, Thea; South African Post Office. June 28, 2007

Clottes, Jean, Ph.D; Archaeologist and author, international rock art authority. June 8, 2007

Gheyle, Woulter, Ph.D; Scientific Researcher, Ghent University, Dept. of Archaeology. June 13, 2007

Olsen, Sandra L., Ph.D; Curator, Carnegie Museum, author. June 29, 2007

Ryder, Oliver A., Ph.D; Kleberg Genetics Chair, Conservation and Research for Endangered Species, Zoological Society of San Diego. June, 4, 2007

Schwartz, Glenn M., Ph.D; Professor of Archaeology, Johns Hopkins University. June 22, 2007

Smith, Andrew; author/educator. June 16, 2007.

Sumner, William; Capt. U.S. Army, archaeologist and Arabian rescuer in Baghdad. June 23, 2007

July 2007
Lahafian, Jamal. Freelance Iraqi rock art researcher.

ARTICLES

Archaeology Magazine News staff, "Fetching Figurines," *Archaeology Magazine*, Mar/Apr 2004.

Arnaud, Bernadette, "Equud on Ice," *Archaeology Magazine*, Jan/Feb 2000.

Barclay, Alistair, "Uffington Horse," *Oxford Archaeology*, 2003.

BBC News staff, "Climate Killed Alaskan Horse," BBC, November 13, 2003.

————, "Foal born to herd of wild horses," BBC, Mar. 16, 2007.

————, "When Birds Ate Horses," BBC, Nov. 14, 2001.

————, "Wild Horses in Kent," BBC, Oct. 21, 2002.

————, "Wild horses to graze city reserve," BBC, Nov. 9, 2006.

Carey, Bjorn, "Humans Wiped Out Wild Horses, Study Says," MSNBC News, May 1, 2006.

CBC News staff, "Alberta Scientists Find Prehistoric Horse, " CBC, May 3, 2001.

Finn, Christine, "Timeless Thoroughbred," *Archaeology Magazine*, Sept/Oct 2001.

Graham, Sarah, "Sculptures Reveal Artistic Mastery of Prehistoric Europeans," *Scientific American*, Dec. 18, 2003.

Handwerk, Brian, "Ice Age Horses May Have Been Killed Off by Humans," *National Geographic News*, May 1, 2006.

Holland, Jennifer Steinberg, "Zebras: Born to Roam," *National Geographic* online.

Joyce, Christopher, "Huge Terror Bird Discovered in Patagonia," National Public Radio, Oct. 25, 2006.

Levine, Marsha A., "Domestication, Breed Diversification and Early History of the Horse," McDonald Institute of Archaeological Research, Cambridge, UK.

Lovett, Richard A., "Ancient Manure May Be Earliest Proof of Horse Domestication," National Geographic, Oct. 26, 2006.

Mayell, Hillary, "Remains Show Ancient Horses Were Hunted for Their Meat," National Geographic News, May 11, 2001.

Mulvey, Stephen, "Wildlife Defies Chernobyl Radiation," BBC, April 20, 2006.

New Scientist News staff, "Humans Back in Time Frame for Horse Extinction," New Scientist, May 2, 2006.

Oscampo, Paul, "Ancient DNA helps clarify the origins of two extinct New World horse species," Innovations Report, June 28,2005.

Owens, James, "Horse Evolution Followed Twisty Trail, Study Shows," National Geographic News, March 17, 2005.

Popsin, Colleen P., "Hunters Horse Around," Archaeology Magazine, Nov/Dec 2002.

Roach, John, "Ancient Figurines Found—From First Modern Humans?," National Geographic News, Dec. 17, 2003.

Romey, Kristin M., "All that Glitters is Scythian," Archaeology Magazine, Jan/Feb 2000.

Samashev, Zainullah, "Scythian Steeds," Archaeology Magazine, May/June 2002.

Science Daily News staff, "Clues to Horse Extinction Point to Gritty Grass, Climate Change," Science Daily, October 20, 1997.

———, "New Evidence of Early Horse Domestication," Science Daily, Nov. 3, 2006.

BOOKS

Clottes, Jean; Bahn, Paul G. (translated by). Chauvet Cave: The Art of Earliest Times. Salt Lake City, University of Utah Press, 2003

Dixon, Dougal and others. The Macmillan Illustrated Encyclopedia of Dinosaurs and Prehistoric Animals: A Visual Who's Who of Prehistoric Life. New York, Collier Books, Macmillan Publishing Co., 1998.

Hausman, Gerald and Loretta. *The Mythology of Horses: Horse Legend and Love Throughout the Ages*. New York, Three Rivers Press, 2003.

Horse Capture, George P. *A Song for the Horse Nation: Native American Culture*. Golden, CO, Fulcrum Publishing, 2006

Olsen, Sandra L. PhD, *Horses through Time*. Lanham, MD, Roberts Rinehart, 2003

Ransford, Sandy. *The Kingfisher Illustrated Horse & Pony Encyclopedia*. Boston, MA, Kingfisher, 2004

White, Randall. *Prehistoric Art: The Symbolic Journey of Humankind*. New York, Harry N. Abrahms, Inc, Publisher, 2003.

WEB SITES

Academy of Natural Science—Thomas Jefferson's fossil collection
http://www.ansp.org/museum/jefferson/index.php

Art and Archaeology
http://www.art-and-archaeology.com/india/bhi4.html

Arts Council of Korea—rock art
http://www.arko.or.kr/home2005/eng2007/index.jsp

Asian Art.com—rock art and sculptures
http://www.asianart.com/articles/

Berkshire History.Com, The Uffington White Horse
http://www.berkshirehistory.com/archaeology/white_horse.html

Bradshaw Foundation: Cosquer Cave
http://www.bradshawfoundation.com/cosquer/cosquer3.html

Cave Chauvet Pont d' Arc
http://www.culture.gouv.fr/culture/arcnat/chauvet/en/

Conquistador Magazine
http://www.conquistador.com/index.html

Domestication, Breed Diversification and Early History of the Horse
http://www3.vet.upenn.edu/labs/equinebehavior//hvnwkshp/hv02/levine.htm

Florida Museum of Natural History Fossil Horse Cyber Museum
http://www.flmnh.ufl.edu/natsci/vertpaleo/fhc/firstCM.htm

Hagerman Fossil Beds National Park
http://www.nps.gov/hafo/

Iberian Horses
http://lusitanohorse.josefonteslusitanos.com/iberian-horses.htm

Ice Age Art: Vogelherd, Germany
http://www.ice-age-art.de/anfaenge_der_kunst/vogelherd.php

John Day Fossil Beds National Park
http://www.nps.gov/joda/index.htm

Kentucky Horse Park: International Museum of the Horse
http://www.ket.org/artofthehorse/

MET Museum
http://www.metmuseum.org/

Naturhistorisches Museum Mainz, Eckfeld Maar Crater
http://www.eckfelder-maar.de/welcomee.htm

Niaux
http://www.niaux.net/

Oklahoma State University Dept. of Agriculture
http://www.ansi.okstate.edu/

Page Museum, La Brea Tar Pits
http://www.tarpits.org/

Perlino in Icelandic horses
http://www.icelandichorse.is/perlino.html

San Diego Zoo
http://www.sandiegozoo.org/

University of Tubingin
http://www.uni-tuebingen.de/allcach2002?sflag=soc

Wild Horses: An American Romance
http://net.unl.edu/artsFeat/wildhorses/wildintro.html

Yukon Beringia Interpretive Center
http://www.beringia.com/02/02maina14.html

INDEX